AGAIN THE FAR MORNING

AGAIN
THE FAR

MORNING

NEW AND SELECTED POEMS

N. Scott Momaday

UNIVERSITY OF NEW MEXICO PRESS   ALBUQUERQUE

First paperbound printing, 2013

Paperbound ISBN: 978-0-8263-4843-2

17 16 15 14 13   1 2 3 4 5

Library of Congress Cataloging-in-Publication Data

Momaday, N. Scott, 1934–

Again the far morning : new and selected poems / N. Scott Momaday.

p. cm.

ISBN 978-0-8263-4842-5 (cloth : alk. paper)

I. Title.

ps3563.o47A73 2011

811′.54—dc22

2010028435

Design and composition: Melissa Tandysh

To Barbara

For the bright, unlikely world she made

CONTENTS

IN THE BEAR'S HOUSE, 1999

NEW POEMS

PREFACE

I believe that the poem is the highest form of verbal expression. We most often think of the poem as a composition in writing, but it may also be spoken or sung. The earliest poems belong to what is called the oral tradition; that is, they were transmitted by the human voice. We are told that writing is about six thousand years old. The oral tradition is inestimably older, as old as language itself.

"Form" is the operative word in the first sentence above. I have written in various forms of literature—novels, plays, essays, travel—and I have written in various forms of poetry. In the strict sense poems are distinguished from prose in that they are composed in verse, iambic pentameter presumably being the normal beat and measure of the English language. But there are definitive poetic elements apart from verse. Though perhaps more tentative, a poem may be a poem by virtue of its rhythm, alliteration, imagery, precision, etc. Thus terms such as "free verse" and "prose poem," which may appear to be contradictions in terms, are valid within their frame of reference.

The oral tradition of the American Indian is very important to me, and it has informed much of my writing. The poem, in the strict sense of the word, does not exist in that tradition, but song and story are indispensable and highly developed. Both are infused with poetic character. Moreover, the song in oral tradition is invested with a belief in the intrinsic power of language. That power is definitive, and it informs the best of poems. My Kiowa father sang and told stories to me from the Kiowa oral tradition from the time I was a young child. That tradition has been largely influential in the determination of my literary voice. My mother, who was predominately English, was a writer, and she gave me a deep love of, and respect for, the English language.

My principal objective as a poet is to write directly from my mind and heart in the traditions that are my heritage. To trade in the wonder of words and to be acquainted with those whose best expressions have sustained us, that is literature.

—N. Scott Momaday

ANGLE OF GEESE
1974

Before an Old Painting of the Crucifixion

I ponder how He died, despairing once.
I've heard the cry subside in vacant skies,
In clearings where no other was. Despair,
Which in the vibrant wake of utterance,
Resides in desolate calm, preoccupies.
Though it is still. There is no solace there.

That calm inhabits wilderness, the sea,
And where no peace inheres but solitude;
Near death it most impends. It was for Him,
Absurd and public in His agony,
Inscrutably itself, nor misconstrued,
Nor metaphrased in art or pseudonym:

A vague contagion. Old, the mural fades . . .
Reminded of the fainter sea I scanned,
I recollect: How mute in constancy!
I could not leave the wall of palisades
Till cormorants returned my eyes on land.
The mural but implies eternity.

Not death, but silence after death is change.
Judean hills, the endless afternoon,
The farther groves and arbors seasonless
But fix the mind within the moment's range.
Where evening would obscure our sorrow soon,
There shines too much a sterile loveliness.

No imprecisions of commingled shade,
No shimmering deceptions of the sun.
Herein no semblances remark the cold
Unhindered swell of time, for time is stayed.
The Passion wanes into oblivion.
And time and timelessness confuse, I'm told.

These centuries removed from either fact
Have lain upon the critical expanse
And been of little consequence. The void
Is calendared in stone; the human act,
Outrageous, is in vain. The hours advance
Like flecks of foam borne landward and destroyed.

The Bear

What ruse of vision,
escarping the wall of leaves,
rending incision
into countless surfaces,

Would cull and color
his somnolence, whose old age
has outworn valor,
all but the fact of courage?

Seen, he does not come,
move, but seems forever there,
dimensionless, dumb,
in the windless noon's hot glare.

More scarred than others
these years since the trap maimed him,
plain slants his withers,
drawing up the crooked limb.

Then he is gone, whole,
without urgency, from sight,
as buzzards control,
imperceptibly, their flight.

Buteo Regalis

His frailty discrete, the rodent turns, looks.
What sense first warns? The winging is unheard,
Unseen but as distant motion made whole,
Singular, slow, unbroken, in its glide.
It veers, and veering tilts broad-surfaced wings.
Aligned, the span bends to begin the dive
And falls, alternately white and russet,
Angle and curve, gathering momentum.

Earth and I Gave You Turquoise

Earth and I gave you turquoise
When you walked singing
We lived laughing in my house
And told old stories
You grew ill when the owl cried
We will meet on Black Mountain
I will bring corn for planting
And we will make fire
Children will come to your breast
You will heal my heart
I speak your name many times
The wild cane remembers you
My young brother's house is filled
I go there to sing
We have not spoken of you
But our songs are sad
When Moon Woman goes to you
I will follow her white way
Tonight they dance near Chinle
By the seven elms
There your loom whispered beauty
They will eat mutton
And drink coffee till morning
You and I will not be there

Simile

What did we say to each other
That now we are as the deer
Who walk in single file
With heads high
With ears forward
With eyes watchful
With hooves always placed on firm ground
In whose limbs there is latent flight

Plainview 1

There in the hollow of the hills I see,
Eleven magpies stand away from me.

Low light upon the rim; a wind informs
This distance with a gathering of storms

And drifts in silver crescents on the grass,
Configurations that appear, and pass.

There falls a final shadow on the glare,
A stillness on the dark, erratic air.

I do not hear the longer wind that lows
Among the magpies. Silences disclose,

Until no rhythms of unrest remain,
Eleven magpies standing in the plain.

They are illusion—wind and rain revolve—
And they recede in darkness, and dissolve.

The Fear of Bo-talee

Bo-talee rode easily among his enemies, once, twice,
Three and four times. And all who saw him were
Amazed, for he was utterly without fear; so it seemed.
But afterwards he said: Certainly I was afraid. I was
Afraid of the fear in the eyes of my enemies.

The Horse That Died of Shame

*Once there was a man who owned a fine hunting horse. It was black and fast
and afraid of nothing. When it was turned upon an enemy it charged in a
straight line and struck at full speed; the man need have no hand upon the
rein. But, you know, that man knew fear. Once during a charge he turned
that animal from its course. That was a bad thing. The hunting horse died
of shame.*

—FROM *The Way to Rainy Mountain*

In the one color of the horse there were many colors. And that
evening it wheeled, riderless, and broke away into the long
distance, running at full speed. And so it does again and again
in my dreaming. It seems to concentrate all color and light into
the final moment of its life, until it streaks the vision plane and
is indefinite, and shines vaguely like the gathering of March
light to a storm.

The Delight Song of Tsoai-talee

I am a feather in the bright sky.
I am the blue horse that runs in the plain.
I am the fish that rolls, shining in the water.
I am the shadow that follows a child.
I am the evening light, the luster of meadows.
I am an eagle playing with the wind.
I am a cluster of bright beads.
I am the farthest star.
I am the cold of the dawn.
I am the roaring of the rain.
I am the glitter on the crust of the snow.
I am the long track of the moon in a lake.
I am a flame of four colors.
I am a deer standing away in the dusk.
I am a field of sumac and the pomme blanche.
I am an angle of geese upon the winter sky.
I am the hunger of a young wolf.
I am the whole dream of these things.
You see, I am alive, I am alive
I stand in good relation to the earth.
I stand in good relation to the gods.
I stand in good relation to all that is beautiful.
I stand in good relation to the daughter of Tsen-tainte.
You see, I am alive, I am alive.

Headwaters

Noon in the intermountain plain:
There is scant telling of the marsh—
A log, hollow and weather-stained,
An insect at the mouth, and moss—
Yet waters rise against the roots,
Stand brimming to the stalks. What moves?
What moves on this archaic force
Was wild and welling at the source.

Rainy Mountain Cemetery

Most is your name the name of this dark stone.
Deranged in death, the mind to be inheres
Forever in the nominal unknown,
The wake of nothing audible he hears
Who listens here and now to hear your name.

The early sun, red as a hunter's moon,
Runs in the plain. The mountain burns and shine;
And silence is the long approach of noon
Upon the shadow that your name defines—
And death this cold, black density of stone.

Angle of Geese

How shall we adorn
Recognition with our speech?—
　　Now the dead firstborn
Will lag in the wake of words

　　Custom intervenes;
We are civil, something more:
　　More than language means,
The mute presence mulls and marks.

　　Almost of a mind,
We take measure of the loss;
　　I am slow to find
The mere margin of repose.

　　And one November
It was longer in the watch,
　　As if forever,
Of the huge ancestral goose.

　　So much symmetry!
Like the pale angle of time
　　And eternity.
The great shape labored and fell.

　　Quit of hope and hurt,
It held a motionless gaze,
　　Wide of time, alert,
On the dark distant flurry.

THE GOURD DANCER
1976

The Colors of Night

1. WHITE

An old man's son was killed far away in the Staked Plains. When the old man heard of it he went there and gathered up the bones. Thereafter, wherever the old man ventured, he led a dark hunting horse which bore the bones of his son on its back. And the old man said to whomever he saw: "You see how it is that now my son consists in his bones, that his bones are polished and so gleam like glass in the light of the sun and moon, that he is very beautiful."

2. YELLOW

There was a boy who drowned in the river, near the grove of thirty-two bois d'arc trees. The light of the moon lay like a path on the water, and a glitter of low brilliance shone in it. The boy looked at it and was enchanted. He began to sing a song that he had never heard before; only then, once, did he hear it in his heart, and it was borne like a cloud of down upon his voice. His voice entered into the bright track of the moon, and he followed after it. For a time he made his way along the path of the moon, singing. He paddled with his arms and legs and felt his body rocking down into the swirling water. His vision ran along the path of light and reached across the wide night and took hold of the moon. And across the river, where the path led into the shadows of the bank, a black dog emerged from the river, shivering and shaking the water from its hair. All night it stood in the waves of the grass and howled the full moon down.

3. BROWN

On the night before a flood, the terrapins move to high ground. How is it that they know? Once there was a boy who took up a terrapin in his hands and looked at it for a long time, as hard as he could look. He succeeded in memorizing the terrapin's face, but he failed to see how it was that the terrapin knew anything at all.

4. RED

There was a man who had got possession of a powerful medicine. And by means of this medicine he made a woman out of sumac leaves and lived with her for a time. Her eyes flashed, and her skin shone like pipestone. But the man abused her, and so his medicine failed. The woman was caught up in a whirlwind and blown apart. Then nothing was left of her but a thousand withered leaves scattered in the plain.

5. GREEN

A young girl awoke one night and looked out into the moonlit meadow. There appeared to be a tree; but it was only an appearance; there was a shape made of smoke; but it was only an appearance; there was a tree.

6. BLUE

One night there appeared a child in the camp. No one had ever seen it before. It was not bad-looking, and it spoke a language that was pleasant to hear, though none could understand it. The wonderful thing was that the child was perfectly unafraid, as if it were at home among its own people. The child got on well enough, but the next morning it was gone, as suddenly as it had appeared. Everyone was troubled. But then it came to be understood that the child never was, and everyone felt better. "After all," said an old man, "how can we believe in the child? It gave us not one word of sense to hold on to. What we saw, if indeed we saw anything at all, must have been a dog from a neighboring camp, or a bear that wandered down from the high country."

7. PURPLE

There was a man who killed a buffalo bull to no purpose, only he wanted its blood on his hands. It was a great, old, noble beast, and it was a long time blowing its life away. On the edge of the night the people gathered themselves up in their grief and shame. Away in the west they could see the hump and spine of a huge beast which lay dying along the edge of the world. They could see its bright blood run into the sky, where it dried, darkening, and was at last flecked with flakes of light.

8. BLACK

There was a woman whose hair was long and heavy and black and beautiful. She drew it about her like a shawl and so divided herself from the world that not even Age could find her. Now and then she steals into the men's societies and fits her voice into their holiest songs. And always, just there, is a shadow which the firelight cannot cleave.

The Monoliths

The wind lay upon me.
The monoliths were there
In the long light, standing
Cleanly apart from time.

For the Old Man for Drawing
Dead at Eighty-Nine

... at ninety I shall have penetrated
To the essence of all things ...
—HOKUSAI

This late drawing:
In these deft lines
A corpulent merchant reclines
Against a pillow.
Here is a fragile equation
For which there is an Asian origin.
In this and that and another stroke
There is something like possibility
Succeeding into infinity.
In another year there might have been here
Not apparently
A corpulent merchant and his pillow
But really
Three long winds converging on the dawn.

Abstract: Old Woman in a Room

For Olga Sergeevna Akhmanova

Here is no place of easy consequence
But where you come to reckon recompense;

And here the vacancy in which are met
The vague contingencies of your regret.

Here is the will's disease. And otherwise
Here is no reparation in surmise.

Here the white light that touches your white hair.
Replaces you in darkness and despair.

And here where age constricts you, death is dear,
And essences of anguish stay you here.

The Burning

In the numb, numberless days
There were disasters in the distance,
Strange upheavals. No one understood them.
At night the sky was scored with light,
For the far planes of the planet buckled and burned.
In the dawns were intervals of darkness
On the scorched sky, clusters of clouds and eclipse,
And cinders descending.
Nearer in the noons
The air lay low and ominous and inert.
And eventually at evening, or morning, or midday,
At the sheer wall of the wood,
Were shapes in the shadows approaching,
Always, and always alien and alike.
And in the foreground the fields were fixed in fire,
And the flames flowered in our flesh.

The Wound

The wound gaped open;
It was remarkably like the wedge of an orange
When it is split, spurting.
He wanted to close the wound with a kiss,
To graft his mouth to the warm, wet tissue.
He kept about the wound, waiting
And deeply disturbed,
His fascination
Like the inside of the wound itself,
Deep, as deep almost as the life principle,
The irresistible force of being.
The force lay there in the rupture of the flesh,
There in the center of the wound.

Had he been God,
He should himself have inflicted the wound;
And he should have taken the wound gently,
Gently in his hands, and placed it
Among the most brilliant wildflowers
In the meadows of the mountains.

Forms of the Earth at Abiquiu

For Georgia O'Keeffe

I imagine the time of our meeting
There among the forms of the earth at Abiquiu,
And other times that followed from the one—
An easy contrivance of stories,
And late luncheons of wine and cheese.
All around there were beautiful objects,
Clean and precise in their beauty, like bone.
Indeed, bone: a snake in the filaments of bone,
The skulls of cows and sheep;
And the many smooth stones in the window,
In the flat winter light, were beautiful.
I wanted to feel the sun in the stones—
The ashen, far-flung winter sun—
But this I did not tell you, I believe,
But I believe that after all you knew.
And then, in those days, too
I made you the gift of a small, brown stone,
And you described it with the tips of your fingers
And knew at once that it was beautiful—
At once, accordingly you knew,
As you knew the forms of the earth at Abiquiu:
That time involves them and they bear away,
Beautiful, various, remote,
In failing light, and the coming of cold.

The Gift

For Bobby Jack Nelson

Older, more generous,
We give each other hope.
The gift is ominous:
Enough praise, enough rope.

Simile

What did we say to each other
that now we are as the deer
who walk in single file
with heads high
with ears forward
with eyes watchful
with hooves always placed on
                    firm ground
in whose limbs there is
                    latent flight

Rhymes for Emily

She wrote with such ungodly
                    haste,
You'd think there'd be a ton
                    of waste
Fact is, she listened to the bird
And learned the thittering
                    of words.

Plainview 1

Three in the hollow of the hills I see,
Eleven magpies stand away from me.

Low light upon the hills; a wind informs
This distance with a gathering of storms
And drifts in silver crescents in the grass,
Configurations that appear, and pass.

The faces & final shadow in the glass.
A stillness on the dark, creative air

I do not hear the longer wind this leaves
Among the magpies. Silences disclose,
Until no rhythm of concealed remain,
Eleven magpies standing in the plain.

They an illusion — wild & rain revolve —
feel they recede in darkness, and dissolve.

Plainview 3

The sun appearing
                    a pendant
ot clear embers, flashing;
a drift of pollen
                    and glitter
looping and overlapping
                    night:
a prairie fire

The Enquiries

These future Moon in the Ulanghun
Who are they?

Death & Death's dog, Time

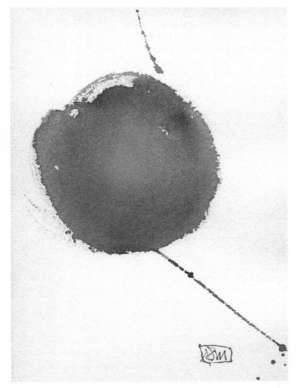

The Bear

What sense or vision,
escaping the wall of leaves,
rends in mirror
into colorless sky-green.

Wonder, such as color,
his astonishment, is how old age
No inborn color,
but the fret of courage?

Seen she does she can
shore, but seems forever there.
dimensionless, durable
in the wilderness howls his glare

More scarred than others,
they scurry over the trees around him,
Paw silents his leather,
drawing up the cracked limbs.

Then he is gone, wholly,
without warning, from sight,
or buzzard control,
in perceptibly their flight,

The Mute Intensity of Love
for Barbara

If only I could tell you what you are
And mean to me, I would as well be done
With speech. My urgent words would carry far
Beyond intent and purpose. Only one
Expression would endure thereof, a sigh
And silence all but inarticulate,
The ancient languages of wind comply
With this communion, this perpetual estate.
For every syllable the heart disdains,
The mute intensity of love remains.

Anywhere is a street
into the Night

Desire will come of waiting
Here at this window — I bring
for she urgency to bear
Upon me, and anywhere
is a street into the night,
Deliverance and delight —
And evenly it will pass
Light this image on the glass.

The Majesty of Relics

How gaunt will be my silence when
You look upon my naked bone,
Reflect upon my grace & then
Subvert my meaning to your own.

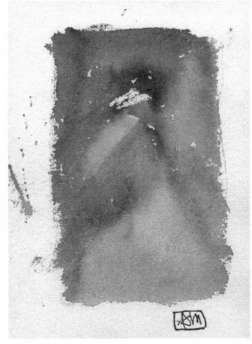

IN THE PRESENCE OF THE SUN
1992

The Gourd Dancer

Mammedaty, 1880–1932

1. THE OMEN
Another season centers on this place.
Like memory the blood congeals in it;
Like memory the sun recedes in time
Into the hazy, southern distances.

A vagrant heat hangs on the dark river,
And shadows turn like smoke. And owl ascends
Among the branches, clattering, remote
Within its motion, intricate with age.

2. THE DREAM
Mammedaty saw to the building of this house. Just
there, by the arbor, he made a camp in the old way.
and in the evening when the hammers had fallen silent
and there were frogs and crickets in the black grass—
and a low hectic wind upon the pale, slanting plane
of the moon's light—he settled deep down in his
mind dream. He dreamed of dreaming, and of the
summer breaking upon his spirit, as drums break upon
the intervals of the dance, and of the gleaming gourds.

3. THE DANCE
Dancing,
He dreams, he dreams—
The long wind glances, moves
Forever as a music to the mind;
The gourds are flashes of the sun.
He takes the inward, mincing steps
That conjure old processions and returns.
Dancing,
His moccasins,
His sash and bandolier

Contain him in insignia;
His fan is powerful, concise
According to his agile hand,
And holds upon the deep, ancestral air.

4. THE GIVEAWAY
Someone spoke his name, Mammedaty, in which
his essence was and is. It was a serious matter that his
name should be spoken there in the circle, among the
many people, and he was thoughtful, full of wonder,
and aware of himself and of his name. He walked
slowly to the summons, looking into the eyes of the man
who summoned him. For a moment they held each
other in close regard and all about them there was
excitement and suspense.

Then a boy came suddenly into the circle, leading
a black horse. The boy ran, and the horse after him.
He brought the horse up short in front of Mammedaty,
and the horse wheeled and threw its head and cut
its eyes in the wild way. And it blew hard and quivered
in its hide so that light ran, rippling, upon its shoulders
and its flanks—and then it stood still and was calm.
Its mane and tail were fixed in braids and feathers, and
a bright red chief's blanket was draped in a roll over
its withers. The boy placed the reins in Mammedaty's
hands. And all of this was for Mammedaty, in his honor,
as even now it is in the telling, and will be, as long as
there are those who imagine him in his name.

The Stalker

Sampt'e drew the string back and back until he
Felt the bow wobble in his hand, and he let the
Arrow go. It shot across the long light of the
Morning and struck the black face of stone in the
Meadow; it glanced then away towards the west,
Limping along in the air; and then it settled down
In the grass and lay still. Sampt'e approached; he
Looked at it with wonder and was wary; honestly he
Believed that the arrow might take flight again;
So much of his life did he give into it.

Long Shadows at Dulce

1.
September is a long
Illusion of itself;
The elders bide their time.

2.
The sheep camps are lively
With children. The slim girls,
The limber girls, recline.

3.
November is the flesh
And the blood of the black bear,
Dusk its bone and marrow.

4.
In the huddled horses
That know of perfect cold
There is calm, like sorrow.

Crows in a Winter Composition

This morning the snow,
The soft distances
Beyond the trees
In which nothing appeared—
Nothing appeared.
The several silences,
Imposed one upon another,
Were unintelligible.

I was therefore ill at ease
When the crows came down,
Whirling down and calling,
Into the yard below
And stood in a mindless manner
On the gray, luminous crust,
Altogether definite, composed,
In the bright enmity of my regard,
In the hard nature of crows.

Planned Parenthood

If coupling should but make us whole
And of the selfsame mind and soul,
Then couple let's in celebration;
We have contained the population.

The Great Fillmore Street
Buffalo Drive

Insinuate the sun through fog
upon Pacific Heights, upon the man on horseback,
upon the herd ascending. There is color and clamor.

And there he waves them down,
those great, humpbacked animals,
until their wild grace gone
they lumber and lunge
and blood blisters at their teeth,
and their hooves score the street—
and among boulders they settle on the sea.

He looks after them, twisted round upon his sorrow,
the drape of his flag now full and formal,
ceremonial.

One bull, animal representation of the sun,
he dreams back from the brink
to the green refuge of his hunter's heart.
It grazes near a canyon wall,
along a ribbon of light, among redbud trees,
eventually into shadow.
Then the hold of his eyes is broken:
on the farther rim the grasses flicker and blur,
a hawk brushes rain across the dusk,
meadows recede into mountains, and here and there
are moons like salmonberries
upon the glacial face of the sky.

Nous avons vu la mer

We have been lovers,
you and I.
We have been alive
in the clear mornings of Genesis;
in the afternoons,
among the prisms of the air,
our hands have shaped perfect silences.
We have seen the sea;
wonder is well known to us.

Wreckage

Had my bones, like the sun,
been splintered on this canyon wall
and burned among these buckled plates,
this bright debris; had it been so,
I should not have lingered so long
among my losses. I should have come
loudly, like a warrior, to my time.

Old Guerre

For Janet

Bertrande: Is he not aged?
Catherine: Yes, Mistress. Greatly aged.
Bertrande: Resentment burdens the heart.
Catherine: And the body keeps time with the heart.

Against his will old Guerre thinks of his son;
You gall me, and I am grown old. You never were.
But, yes, you were. Maybe you are, among soldiers and thieves,
Monks and whores, men of public trust, actors and clowns.
I must not think of you, whom God and I have damned—
It is enough my cloak remarks my daughter's hand.
She bears the contagion of your abandonment
As if it were a season on the fields, sunlight and dust,
Cloudbursts and cold, those things that do permit at last
Of harvests. Bertrande, the same shame encloses us.

I shall go now across the way. In the valley
In the long reach of the snow, I shall lift up my head.
May you and Sanxi find me, small in the country,
And sign me back farewell. And I too shall disappear.

The Hotel 1829

Dusk—and the shimmer of the sea
Has quickened and gone still. The large,
Lithe hurricane birds soar in circles
Beyond the bay, and filmy flamboyants
Stand on the green embankment wavering.

A goat saunters in the street. Its eyes
Gleam in the headlamps like amber
Held up to the moon. Curious,
Seeming not to see, they remain
In after images. She finds them
In the wine, the bright crystal
        At her place.

The glitter on the fog is rain;
And in rainy reach, the long beach curves
Out on the glosses, the vault of lights.
She sees oysters shining in their shells.
Her hand on the hard linen, in candlelight,
        Expresses her.

In a reflected arc the goat's eyes,
In the goat's eyes a random will—and
The late, faint shimmer on the sea.

Great white ships roll in the harbor, illumined
And gracious to the night, their ornaments
Burn on the blur beyond the Hotel 1829.

Concession

Believe the sullen sense that sickness made,
And broke you in its hands.

Believe that death inhabits the mere shade
Intimacy demands.

I drink, my love, to your profound disease;
Its was the better suit.

I could not have provided you this ease,
Nor this peace, absolute.

Woman Waiting on a Porch

Hot and slovenly,
You imagine moving
Towards a bleaker light,
An emptiness.

Go. The soft red morning
Touches strife to your blood.
You imagine
Quiet and ice,

Enough to close
Accounts too lately here,
A dipping of the moon
To the black, jagged range.

Four Charms

1.

My child,
Can you reach those berries,
The red and blue and purple berries?
They are delicious perhaps.

2.

The bear is coming.
There are pitiful cries.
There are knives for mourning.

The bear is coming.
There are bones all about.
There are entrails on the ground.

The bear is coming.
Someone very old has said so.

3.

At the very sight of my horse,
At the very sight of my trappings,
At the very sight of my shield,
You are afraid, aren't you?

4.

The wind is cold,
Isn't it?
The moon is dark,
Isn't it?
The plain is wide,
Isn't it?

Death dances at the base of that hill.

Rings of Bone

There were rings of bone
On the bandoliers of old men dancing.

Then, in the afternoon stippled with leaves
And the shadows of leaves,
The leaves glistened
And their shine shaped the air.

Now the leaves are dead.
Cold comes upon the leaves
And they are crisped upon the stony ground.
Webs of rime, like leaves, fasten on the mould,
And the wind divides and devours the leaves.

Again the leaves have more or less to do
With time. Music pervades the death of leaves.
The leaves clatter like the rings of bone
On the bandoliers of old men dancing.

If It Could Ascend

I behold there
The far, faint motion of leaves.
The leaves shine,
And they will shiver down to death.
Something like a leaf lies here within me;
It wavers almost not at all,
And there is no light to see it by—
That it withers upon a black field.
If it could ascend the thousand years into my mouth,
I would make a word of it at last,
And I would speak it into the silence of the sun.

My Words Do Not Hold

For my father

My words do not hold,
For I am dead.
Nothing remains of me now—
Nothing now.
I am not there in the range of time,
And my fine hands
Do not make the signs
That meant my love,
That drew respect, that struck fear.

Do you hear?—
My breath ravels on the spool of winter.

Listen:
My words do not hold.
My face darkens in the awful turning,
And,
Listening to the winds that wheel away,
You ask after me
And hear only the winds wheeling.

Carnegie, Oklahoma, 1919

This afternoon is older
Than the giving of gifts
And the rhythmic scraping of the red earth.
My father's father's name is called,
And the gift horse stutters out, whole,
The whole horizon in its eyes.
In the giveaway is beaded
The blood memories of the fathers and sons.
Oh, there is nothing like this afternoon
In all the miles and years around,
And I am not here,
But, grandfather, father, I am here.

Lawrence Ranch

Lawrence named it Kiowa.
The Lawrence Tree,
Twisted density of black,
Fronts the dawn,

Stakes the silence
Coyotes crack
As they stitch the field.
Light,

Appearing barely
As the thinnest wash,
Seeps from the ridge,
And day breaks

In successions of the sun
Reporting westward
Across the cold, kindled land
Towards Tierra Amarilla.

December 29, 1890

Wounded Knee Creek

In the shine of photographs
Are the slain, frozen and black

On a simple field of snow.
They image ceremony:

Women and children dancing,
Old men prancing, making fun.

In autumn there were songs, long
Since muted in the blizzard.

In the summer the wild buckwheat
Shone like fox fur and quillwork,

And dusk guttered on the creek.
Now in serene attitudes

Of dance, the dead in glossy
Death are drawn in ancient light.

Fort Sill

Set-angia

You were riding in a wagon to the train.
A tree took shape in the distance.

You began to sing; it was more than unseemly.
The words of your song were so powerful
That nothing less than death could contain them.

At times, many years later, I hear the song,
Not as it was, but as it sounds across time.

Oh my warrior! I love you to sing!
The rattle of your breath, rising to the sun,
I hear among the screams of the hunting horses.

At Risk

I played at words.
It was a long season.

Soft syllables,
Images that shimmered,
Intricate etymologies.

They cohered in wonder.
I was enchanted.

My soul was at risk.
I struggled
Towards hurt,
Towards healing,
Towards passion,
Towards peace.

I wheeled in the shadow of a hawk.
Dizziness came upon me;
The turns of time confounded me.

I lay in a cave,
On a floor cured in blood.

Ancient animals danced about me,
Presenting themselves formally,
In masks.

And there was I, among ancient animals,
In the formality of the dance,
Remembering my face in the mirror of masks.

IN THE BEAR'S HOUSE
1999

To an Aged Bear

Hold hard this infirmity.
It defines you. You are old.

Now fix yourself in summer,
In thickets of ripe berries,

And venture towards the ridge
Where you were born. Await there

The setting sun. Be alive
To that old conflagration

One more time. Mortality
Is your shadow and your shade.

Translate yourself to spirit;
Be present on your journey.

Keep to the trees and waters.
Be the singing of the soil.

Via Dolorosa

A spitting snow
Striking adobe walls,
The cleaving of winter.
A prologue to spring.

Ghosts revel in the fields.
Their tracks tracing
Whorls and switchbacks
On caliche.

This year the miracle
Of Easter
Is sung on bare bristles
Of the injured earth.

A grave pilgrim trudges
Under the heft of the cross,
Trailing a bright spatter
Of black blood.

—Santa Fe

The Remembering

They converge in water
That is absorbed in the dark needlework
At their feet.
Light smokes above them,
Piercing the high weave of pines.
The brake is dark but for the low illumination
Of old snow and bracken and the hoar of the hair
Above the withers.
She squats, her throat wound round
And her thick haunches bowed,
Her broad head borne back beneath her shoulder.
Her feet roll in mud, and her eyes behold
His vague advance, his long looming.
From her daybeds she has risen in his nostrils,
Aching thee.
He takes her, rotating his forearms upon her flanks,
Laying his jaw hard along her spine.
She rocks under his weight—
Yield and brace, yield and brace, is staggered—
And her breath, raveled with his breath,
Resembles wind and rain roiling,
And thunder, far away, rolling.
An image, like remembrance, shimmers in his brain:
A great fish, urgent from the bottom,
Rises fast in the channel, breaks the water
And becomes still and iridescent
Momently in the hard hold of the air,
Then plunges into darkness again, and again.

Prayer for Words

My voice restore for me.
—NAVAJO

Here is the wind bending the reeds westward,
The patchwork of morning on gray moraine;

Had I words I could tell of origin,
Of God's hands bloody with birth at first light,
Of my thin squeals in the heat of his breath,
Of the taste of being, the bitterness,
And scents of camasroot and chokecherries.

And, God, if my mute heart expresses me,
I am the rolling thunder and the bursts
Of torrents upon rock, the whispering
Of old leaves, the silence of deep canyons.
I am the rattle of mortality.

I could tell of the splintered sun. I could
Articulate the night sky, had I words.

The Blind Astrologers

Now, at evening, we hear them.
They sheer and shuffle, cracking
Branches and heaving the air.
Always shyly they appear.

In radiance they take shape
Faintly, their great heads hung low
On arcs of age, their dull eyes
Compassing the murky moon.

They sway and impress the earth
With claws. They incise the ice.
Stars of the first magnitude
Pulse the making of their dance.

They ascend the ancient bridge
And lay fishes in our way,
So to feed us and our dogs.
Along the green slant southward

The blind astrologers blaze
The long traces of our quest.
They lead us, dead reckoning
By the suns they cannot see.

We regard them with wonder,
Fear, and sorrow. They mutter
And cry with voices like ours;
They mime a human anguish.

When they take their leave they fade
Through planes and prisms of rain
Into the drifts of story,
Into calendars and names.

Scaffold Bear

Bears love the taste of whiskey.
—ESTHER NAHGAHNUB

Here in this cave of sleep
I know of an animal on the slope.
No one has seen it,
But there are stories.
Juan Reyes dreamed of it too.
It reared against a moonlit cloud
And sundered the dream.
A young girl spoke of it with wonder,
Having heard it scoop the river for its food.

My own story is this:
A good man killed himself.
The next morning a bear, stripped of its hide,
Lay on a scaffold in a range of trees,
Bleeding, breathing faintly.
Its great paws had been removed.
The bear spoke to someone there, perhaps to me,
For in this cave of sleep
I am at home to bears.

—Tucson

Revenant

You are the dark shape I find
On nights of the spilling moon,
Pale in the pool of heaven.
You are spirit, you are that
Which summons me and confirms
My passage. You know my name.
Your ritual dance remarks
The crooked way between me
And the very thing you are:
Mask, essence, and revenant.
You are, as you ever were,
The energy that sustains
My mere despair. And always
You are the dark shape I find.

—Tucson

Notes on a Hunting Scene

The hunt was ended and the hunter cold.

The far incline of fields and taiga extended to the moon, and the bear
Lay lifeless on a sledge.

Unaccountably, a woman began to laugh, and her laughter was like ice
Rattling in a tin cup. Had it been frozen, it would surely have glittered
Like candlelight upon icons.

The hunter trudged to the fire. A wolf howled in the west, and cold
Was the condition of the world at midnight. Owls were ornamental, and
They were ominous. Behind the hunter's eyes were geometries of time
And distance, intersections of sorrow and fatigue. He imagined his
Grandfather fishing through the ice. A fish, when it was hurled into the
Air, froze instantly and made an iridescent arc upon the sky.

The bear had crept on the edge of the taiga, rearing now and then to
Sniff the wind. When the end came, it slumped slowly down and made
Its bed. It died at a moment between the final rattle of its breath and
The awful silence that followed, the moment cannot be fixed exactly in
The range of time.

The woman drank from a bottle and laughed again.

In the village pain was preserved in the way that embers are kept alive.
Life did not persist without pain. Somewhere it is written.

The bear lay lifeless on the sledge. Sooner or later the singer would
Come, and everything would have its place in the relief of ritual.

Winter Solstice at Amoxiumqua

For Barbara

In the village, *ketha'me*
in the canyon, *ketha'me*
in New Mexico, *ketha'me*
a fine snow is falling.

The flakes swirl
as if to discover a wind
purling upon the laden limbs.

To the west
the canyon wall, blacked out,
is nonetheless present and looming.

Upon it lowly remain
the ruins of Amoxiumqua.
Imagine a bear standing
in a street of that ancient town.

There is no moon,
no light by which to see
the fine snow falling.

In the dull memory of its blood
the bear discerns the swirling flakes,
and points of cold
sting its nebulous eyes.

Then, when its wild brain
can no longer conceive of the sun or moon,
the shifting fog becomes almost luminous,
and it conjures, as a gift, the village below.

Meditation on Wilderness

In the evening's orange and umber light,
There come vagrant ducks skidding on the pond.
Together they veer inward to the reeds.
The forest—aspen, oak, and pine—recedes,
And the sky is smudged on the ridge beyond.
There is more in my soul than in my sight.

I would move to the other side of sound;
I would be among the bears, keeping still,
Not watching, waiting instead. I would dream,
And in that old bewilderment would seem
Whole in a beyond of dreams, primal will
Drawn to the center of this dark surround.

The sacred here emerges and abides.
The day burns down, the hours dissolve in time;
The bears parade the deeper continent
As silences pervade the firmament,
And wind wavers on the radiant rime.
Here is the house where wilderness resides.

Seven Photographs of Winter

1.

Here is another season of the air,
An essence other seasons softly bear.
The wind engenders dreams of holiness,
And we are come to goodness, more or less:
To wish you all that you deserve and need,
Good health, good work, good company,
Godspeed.

2.

Munich on the last Christmas of the millennium: What could
be better than a fine repast at Dallmayr, then a stroll through the
Christkindlmarkt in the Marienplatz? The sun is low, casting a rose
and orange glow behind the great domes of the Frauenkirche. The
stalls, filled with sweet edibles, ornaments, and handicrafts from all
of Bavaria glitter in the colored lights. The air is crisp and fragrant
and particular. There are snowflakes on the ascending night.

One concerted sound rises above all others, that of a choir on a
balcony below the great glockenspiel. It seems almost ethereal, some
perfect vibrancy from a world beyond. The great throng of people in
the square are transported. They are as one, a body wholly held in the
trance of music, devotion, solemnity. Their faces are turned upward,
their common humanity borne upon the eternal spirit of this holy
night. Even as it ends, they hold on to the chorus that is now echo,
now void, at last applauding with mittened hands, a tribute that
does not break the silence.

3.

We arrived at the dog camp above the Minto Flats. Through the
afternoon and evening Tekla, age six, extraordinarily pretty and
precocious, and I made friends. We told each other stories. She
interviewed me, writing with keen deliberation in her notebook.
She drew pictures for me. She gave me a stick, wrapped round
with brightly colored yarns, her own artistic creation and a kind

of sacred totem, I believe. She showed me how to set the ice tray, filled with water at room temperature, outside the door, and in fifteen minutes we had ice for lemonade. She showed me how to bring firewood in a sled, how to feed the puppies, and how to bounce her baby sister on the bed. Everything she did was done with charm, imagination, gladness and good will. I was smitten.

The next morning Tekla's mother Susan and I went mushing, I in the basket and Susan on the runners. There was a wonderful silence on the white world, barely broken by the hard patter of the dogs. I watched the team lining out before me, moving in a kind of choreography, bearing us on gusts of pure exhilaration. My eyes, stung by the cold, were tearing. It seemed to me that we were going very fast. Then in my peripheral vision, on the right, there suddenly appeared something close at hand, and I was startled. There, on her own sled, drawn by her own dog, came Tekla gliding past us in a bright blur. She sped away, giggling in the joy of childhood, dissolving into the wall of wilderness. And I was borne there, too, on the sheer edge of wonder.

4.

This year the weather was crisp and clear, of a New Mexican brightness that is like glitter on the air. In January there was a perfect day for the *Matachina*, a Spanish dance that expresses in art the unique amalgamation of Spanish and Indian cultures in the Southwest. When I was a boy I had seen the dance in falling snow and imagined that it could not be more beautiful. But the purity of light this year gave to the costumes of the dancers a brilliance beyond my imagining. The costumes of the *Matachina* are the most colorful of all in Pueblo ceremony—scarves and ribbons of every color, headdresses ornamented with silver and semiprecious stones, tassels of sparkling beadwork, and wands that flash and dazzle in the sun like fireworks or a thousand prisms clustered in the golden glare of winter afternoon. Squash kiva danced to a drum. Turquoise kiva danced to violins, played by descendants of Conquistadors who live in the old Spanish villages nearby. In my boyhood these fiddlers were old men, land grant *labriegos* and *santeros*. This year they were younger men, turned out in the fashion of a rock band, who set up a small amplifier in the plaza, near the shrine of the patron saints. Porcingula and San Diego must have tapped their feet and smiled.

5.

The Christmas orange is not as indispensable, not as definitive as it used to be. To tell the truth, I myself was not, as a boy, filled with awe to find an orange in my stocking. I knew it would be there, after all. (There was no Christmas without it.) And after all an orange is an orange. Nor have my children been especially taken with the Christmas orange. Oranges have come to be ubiquitous, common as burrs, and therefore taken for granted. A fruit for every season.

But think of this. My father was a Native American, a full-blood Kiowa, born in 1913 on the Great Plains in Oklahoma, in the deep interior of the continent. When he was taken as a small child in a wagon to see his first Christmas program at Rainy Mountain Church, he had never seen a Christmas tree, and he had never seen an orange.

When an orange was given to him, and he held it in his hands, he must have been filled with wonder. Here was a beautiful bright ball, of a color that shone like the sun, marvelous to see, cool and textured to the touch. Moreover, when it was opened, like a present from the earth, there was inside a meat fragrant, succulent, tender, full to bursting with a juice so sweet and delicious as to humble his imagination. He would not have another orange until the next Christmas, but he would remember this one, and he would cherish the memory as long as he lived.

My father became a teacher, and he and my mother taught at Jemez Pueblo, New Mexico, for a quarter of a century. The day school there went through the first six grades. Every year, before the Christmas program, my father went to the produce markets in Albuquerque and Santa Fe, and he brought back many good things to eat—and always oranges. No child at the Jemez Day School ever went without a Christmas orange.

I am told that the Three Wise Men brought gifts of gold,
frankincense, and myrrh to the Christchild. I like to think
that the gold might have been an orange, and that the
Christchild might have found it wonderful beyond the telling.

6.

Sometimes when I look along a corridor of the earth, I am aware
that someone, a thousand years ago, saw exactly what I see, for the
rocks and mountains are perpetual calendars, telling the soul's time.
And what is entered there are the numerals of eternity. I see and
come away in humility.

7.

Dark firelight ripples on the frosted glass,
Mere shadows of processions where they pass.

At dawn the sky is like the curdled seas.
The snow transfigures landscape by degrees.

The camera contains the winter world,
The scene is on the lens. The cold is curled

About the solstice, and the range of time
Is broken on the needles and the rime.

Through time exposures are the heavens seen.
Behold with wonder that the moon is green.

A portrait of the family at best
Is that of you and me and all the rest,

And on the picture plane a homely birth,
A holy composition, peace on earth.

The Threads of Odyssey

1.

I dream again the far morning in which the boy comes to me. He takes my hand, and we walk on the edge of the village, along the river. He is more alive than I to the things around us—the sound of the soft wind, the glints of light that dance on the water, the shadows of birds that dart on the canyon walls, the smell of woodsmoke and the feel of the uneven ground beneath our feet. His senses are sharper than mine, and his capacity for wonder greater. The grasp of his small hand is firm. He shares with me his delight and curiosity. He is excited just to be, and his excitement spills over upon me, and I am more sensitive to the world than I was before we touched hands. He has wonder enough for us both.

"Look!" he nearly shouts, and he points to the northern sky, where a great tumbling cloud has appeared on the blue mountain. Had I not been with the boy, it would have seemed an unremarkable sight. But now as I look at it I see how extraordinary and how beautiful it is. And besides, it has the shape of an ice bear; then, roiling, it becomes a dinosaur and then a great mouse. In the long distance, there is a sound of rolling thunder, so low as to be nearly inaudible. We keep a customary silence, the boy and I. I know by his example that silence is the house of the soul.

2.

At midmorning it begins to snow. The sky has descended into the canyon, and the walls are invisible in the mist. It is the first snowfall of the season, and the boy is beside himself with joy. Even before he has put on his coat, cap, and mittens he is in the open doorway, pulling at my arm. Some flakes come swirling into the house, and in the swirl he dances. He is like the crow dancers at Zia who come down from the hills on New Year's Day and beat their feet on the earth in perfect time to the drum. Or he is like a koshare, a small member of the ancient society of clowns, a definition of mischief and mystery and holiness.

I ponder the snow. Each unique flake glides to the earth and is gone. Were it possible to catch just one flake in midair, when it is pierced with sunlight, and hold it under a microscope, there would appear something like a prism, perhaps, but more intricate—or a dreamcatcher, a perfect symmetry, so fragile as to exist on the very edge of existence.

But to the boy the snow is more intrinsic to the world as a whole. He has no need to see with the mind's eye the microscopic particles that are beneath the surface of the visible plane. No matter that he does not see beyond appearances. The apparent world is enough to fill his heart.

3.

So it is that an eagle can focus upon every object in its range of vision simultaneously. I can focus upon one. Oh, but to see, a single object at a time, the world in which I am alive! Surely that is worth dying for; to see clearly the wonders of wilderness and oceans and mountains, that is to earn one's death. And to see the monuments of one's life from the plane of age, that is good. The other day I saw the arbor at the homestead on Rainy Mountain Creek. It is vacant, and it is falling into ruin, and I want with all my heart to save it. Even old and dilapidated, it is beautiful to me, for it is one of the homes of my spirit. There I was brought from birth; there I was given my Indian name; and there, just beyond the northeast corner, my father was born in a tepee. I wonder if the arbor will stand as long as I do.

In the Malpais, the boy sees a double rainbow, very close in the east. It is more brilliant than any rainbow he has seen. And at Lukachukai he steps outside a hogan at night and beholds a sky full of stars. It is a sight that he will never be able to describe in words, but he will keep the vision as long as he lives. It is simply a signature of God, the universe drawn with light, wholly gratuitous and unexpected. In the presence of such things, there is only a still stance of the spirit, a quiet like creation. The boy is here, here in the world, in the embrace of eternity. He leads me to old revelations, those that I knew once upon a time.

4.

On a day such as this, in the far morning, when the wind was cutting and shrill among the bare black limbs of the elms and junipers, and the fields were frozen, the boy thought of what would become of him. The world was a lonely place, but it was full not only of possibility but of promise. He might have been thought of as poor by many—if he was thought of at all—but he thought of himself as a man on a horse, and that vague, enchanted image, that preliminary drawing of a centaur, was enough to define him in his becoming, enough to lift his heart seventeen hands above the ground.

"Who am I?" the boy asks. I have been expecting the question. It is the most important question he, or anyone, can ask. "I don't know," I reply, "or I know only in part. But you must search for the whole answer. It is yours, yours only, to find. That is the object of your life."

He shrugs, eats an apple. I regard him. He is vital, curious, unknowing of his acute vulnerability. Well, so long as he doesn't know. The unknowing gives him a chance.

We breakfast, the boy and I. He seems not to taste his food, but to take it for granted. I think of what a physician once said to me, "food is food." As for me, I savor my toast and eggs. The boy will come to be a maker of imaginative omelets, I think. How can it happen? Perhaps it comes about with the feel of a fresh egg in the hand—the bare beauty and simplicity of it, the sensation of cracking it open, the understanding that it yields sustenance, a thing at once delicious and nourishing. I take an egg from the bowl and hand it to him. He holds it with respect, or suspicion. The two things are indistinguishable in his face. I marvel at things that emerge on the far side of my memory.

Say that I live in motion. I love trees and mountains and the walls of canyons. My heart is touched by the stillness of an early morning. But it is at last the things that move with my blood that excite my imagination. A horse that races in the plain, a river that runs fast, a wind that whips at my eyes, a wedge of migrant geese on the sun: these are my benedictions, the definitions of my migrant soul. Migration. It is a word that lies in my brain like a leaf. It rustles and turns, and it spins, like a weaver's wheel, the threads of odyssey.

72   N. SCOTT MOMADAY

NEW POEMS

There Was a Time

There was a time
I wanted nothing so much as you.
In the rain I loved you, in the hot days.
The corn ripened. We were children of storms
                And of seasons.
We ventured from each other and were lost.
But, oh, those salty songs of the damned!
Death has a green foot,
And we dance like fools.

Anywhere Is a Street into the Night

Desire will come of waiting
Here at this window—I bring
In old urgency and fear
Upon me, and anywhere
Is a street into the night,
Deliverance and delight—
And evenly it will pass
Like this image on the glass

American Ballad

Where do you come from,
And where do you go?
Where do you come from,
My Cotton-eye Joe?

Well, I come from the darkness,
And I come in despair.
I come from the darkness
And again will go there.

Black smoke's arisin',
Yonder comes a train.
Winter's comin' on,
Hear the whistle in the rain.

Down in the valley,
The valley so low,
The rails run to darkness.
To darkness I'll go.

Well, there do you come from,
And there do you go,
For there do you come from,
My Cotton-eye Joe.

The Stones at Carlisle

Here are six rows of children. How
Symmetrical the small array.
The names are dim and distant now.
We come and go, and here they stay.
Please pray they rest, and bless each name,
Then reckon innocence and shame.

The Northern Dawn

At Coppermine I saw the Northern Lights.
They wove a green and purple drapery,
Shimmering in place, seeming to descend.
Nothing could seem more constant, more
Perpetual in pale motion. But brief, ephemeral
They were, mere fringes of the ghostly havoc
That pervades the universe, the silent strings
Of infinity, the colors of music beyond time.

Plainview 3

The sun appearing
a pendant
of clear cutbeads, flashing;
a drip of pollen
and glitter
lapping and overlapping
night:
a prairie fire.

An Ivory Edge

What of those fingers,
Those long lovely hands?
Will you place them so
Upon the linen
Of god, the pristine snow,
And carve old epics
With your story knife?

Division

There is a depth of darkness
In the wild country, days of evening
And the silence of the moon.
I have crept upon the bare ground
Where animals have left their tracks,
And faint cries carry on the summits,
Or sink to silence in the muffled leaves.
Here is the world of wolves and bears
And of old, instinctive being,
So noble and indifferent as to be remote
To human knowing. The scales upon which
We seek a balance measure only a divide.

The Old Cemetery

On this electric evening I come here.
It is a place I know and love and fear.
Returning is a ritual of dread:
I would be elsewhere than among the dead.
Belonging is the compass of my soul,
And here the fractions of my self are whole.
Ancestral whispers echo in my brain.
They weave within me, constant as the rain.
I hear my name; my blood informs this ground
And surges in the lightning all around.
Voices exact a memory of those
Who lie about me. And time will enclose
The void between us. Let no thunder cleave
This fragile union, nor this taking leave.

To You Who Named Me

Kiowa George Poolaw, ?–1938

Indeed you were filled with wonder.
Namegivers walked in wonder then.
You bent your voice to story and
The songs of origin and age.
I must have heard you in my infant sleep.
Or barely waking to the tones
That were ancestral and discreet,
Guttural in the deeper throat,
Run through with sorrow and restraint,
And yet forgiveness and consent,
And somewhere in the syllables
An ancient joy, a welcoming.
Thank you, grandfather, that I am,
In your voice, in my name. *Aho.*

To a Man Among Us

For Robert Henry

You emerge in time and chance
One of us, rude in the rigor of birth.
Uncertain and tentative, sowing seeds of promise
As a boy. And now, as a man, you transcend
The limits of locality. You find your stride.

You see to the horizons. You breathe the air
Of crystalline mornings. You walk in the grasses
Of the plains, along the red banks of rivers,
In the foothills of the turning earth.
In scripture and verse you are at home.

You ascend the stair of justice
And take your place among those
Who have fashioned the bulwarks of civilization.
We wish you well and Godspeed. Be of cheer
In your going. Be the keeper of right and rule.

Rhymes for Emily

She wrote with such ungodly haste,
You'd think there'd be a ton of waste.
Fact is, she listened to the birds
And learned the twittering of words.

For Unborn Children

I am.
And knowing how to be,
I am among those who are.
We are old and poor in our existence.
But we make gifts
For those who will become.

Spectre

How faint her humble form
Suspended there among the stars.
She wears the mantle of a mendicant,
Blue or black and meager against the cold.
At her throat the winding of a shroud
Extends the pallor of her face
Into the water hue of her hair.
She bears no expression,
But a silence pulses at her lips
Like lost whispers of the Magdalen.
She stands in the glitter of God,
Against disclosure and the chill of heaven.

Keahdinekeah, Her Hands

          I remember
My great-grandmother's hands.
They were narrow and gnarled
And weak, with no grasp at all.
Mostly they were soft, so soft
That I could not imagine them
Taut and strong as those
Of a woman who held the reins
Of racing horses, who raised
Camps on the windburned plains,
Who handled horns and hides.
I am long removed from her,
But her being is bled into mine,
And I keep the bleak memory
Of her way, and the give-away
Of blood and bone.
          Great-grandmother,
Be for me the long way backward
And the blind way ahead. I am
A tracker of the lost herds.
          In the deep memory
You are whole and vital. I am
Your shadow, marking the ruse
Of time. We are children of the sun.
In the holy riddles, we endure.
          Gladly I remember,
In your little, trembling hands
There was lightly held a gathering
Of many years: old men singing,
Children stamping the ochre earth,
Magpies drifting in fields of snow,
Thunder rolling, and among
The dark saddles of the Wichitas
The howling of wolves ascending
To a hunter's moon.

The Passage Between

Because it's there.

—G. H. L. MALLORY

—a passage outside the range of imagination,
but within the range of experience.

—ISAK DINESEN

The sheer face lay opposite,
Both over and under him.
His lungs burned in the ascent.
His eyes congealed in the cold,
And at last he could not see.
Or what he saw was nothing,
An ice that reflected death,
Present and invisible.
Below he had imagined
The summit within his reach;
He could not imagine now.
There was only the descent
Into mere experience
And the blind passage between.

For Wilma Mankiller, an Honor Song

Your spirit is known to the earth.
You are worthy of great renown.
      The river knows of your spirit,
      The forest knows of your spirit,
      The mountain knows of your spirit,
      The prairie knows of your spirit.
Your spirit is known to the earth.

Your spirit is known to the animals.
You are worthy of great renown.
      The eagle knows of your spirit,
      The bear knows of your spirit,
      The wolf knows of your spirit.
      The mountain lion knows of your spirit.
Your spirit is known to the animals.

Your spirit is known to those who now welcome you.
Let them keep you safe in their camp forever.
We who follow, let us sing and dance in your honor.

Suzdal

Wind in the broad blades,
Bent figures in the fields,
Low walls of an ancient kremlin,
In the rare, rude splendor
Of old Russia, I am young;
I am the singer who sang there.

The Galleries

Do you sense them there, the ones
Who invented art, who saw
That we might see? They linger
Now within these galleries,
Mute, marginal in their minds,
And surpassing in their touch.

What masterpieces they wrought,
Images that leapt through time,
Engulfed in the perfect night
Of millennia and cold,
Skeletal stillness, pending,
Closer than the walls around.

How did they reckon future,
Indeed immortality?
The primal forms they imaged
Yet proceed from some beyond.
They remain, undivided
From the dead and present hand.

A Sloven

A sloven entered the parade,
Was out of step and wanted aid
To fashion well a bold charade.

"I am the Emperor Norton."
His cry was heard by everyone,
From Candlestick to Tiburon.

None questioned his high majesty
Nor did gainsay his sovereignty.
His subjects set his spirit free.

The sloven tarried and held sway
Until at last he passed away
And into legend by the Bay.

Far in the Flaxen Fields

In the mute morning
The reaper walked to the west,
Shifting from time to time
The shimmering scythe
That swung like a pendulum
From the ascending sun.
At Midday he had got
Far in the flaxen fields.
Striding then in the tapered shade
He seemed to cleave the day
Downward from the blind meridian.
And in the soft sight of a bear,
He merged with the wall of woods
And the green pale of genesis.

The New River Northward

The river runs steadily northward,
Clear and intricate with shade.
On the near bank stands a great tree,
The branches white and stark just now,
Not yet greening into spring.
Ten years ago I placed an offering
In the narrow fork of the tree,
And I said a rude, immediate prayer.
Now the softest echoes of the words
Run slowly northward, year after year,
And the river flows beneath facets
Of green and gray light northward.

From the River House I see the tree,
And I am moved to regard it with respect.
It stands in the presence of my mind,
After all, aging as I age, involving me
In the keeping of the river and the land.
The river runs northward through time,
And we stay, the tree and I, marking
The passage of drift and dreams.

The Snow Mare

In my dream, a blue mare loping,
Pewter on a porcelain field, away.
There are bursts of soft commotion
Where her hooves drive in the drifts,
And as dusk ebbs on the plane of night,
She shears the web of winter,
And on the far, blind side
She is no more. I behold nothing,
Wherein the mare dissolves in memory,
Beyond the burden of being.

Blood Memory

Palo Duro Canyon

Forever are those days within my reach,
The days of devastation, each by each.
My ghosts recount them in their broken speech.

Meadows of Brit

Are we to live
In precincts of the sun?
Are we to give
Allegiance to the One,

The Lord of light
Who ranges on the sky,
And in the night
Lies low and does not die.

Are we to burn
In waves of solar seas?
Then let us learn
To be and to believe.

Broken Drum's Coup Song

You would do well to turn and run.
I am descended from the sun.
Announce me then and have it done.
Say to your chiefs I am the one.

Beware my father's burning breath;
It is an omen of your death.
I am descended from the sun.
Say to your chiefs I am the one.

Now to Believe

Now to believe that we shall be
Careless again in Brittany,
And married in a chapel there,
And on to sleep in County Clare.

We kissed in rings of standing stones
And breakfasted on tea and scones.
Musicians played for our delight,
And Druids chanted in the night.

In those high moments were we come
To all that we could dream, then some.
And in dimensions of the spheres
We have invested precious years.

The Cave Children

These are the animal's envoys,
The feral girls and bestial boys
Who cull a language from mere noise.

The Bloom of Appearances

Around a nucleus of reality
There is the vacancy of clouds.
Nearly opaque the massive forms,
But they are vagrant and beyond.
There is no substance, only show,
A blooming of appearances.
Rain falls in the troughs of oceans,
And light, as through a prism,
Imposes arcs of color
On the unreality of clouds.
One sees them, and they sail
In sterile, steady winds. And there,
In the vague dimension of illusion,
They cast empty shadows on the earth.

Perfect, More or Less

Nothing is perfect, so you said,
And yet I've measured you in bed.
I know perfection when it comes.
I know your parts, indeed your sums.
More nearly perfect you are not
For more and nearly miss the spot.
The sweet spot that I've come to know
Is more than nearly perfect, oh!

Dear Cousin Em

She is one of those who
Still *write* letters. She informs
Each stroke of the pen
With love. "Dear cousin Em."
There are four pages in all,
A number she deems proper.
She tells of the coming of spring,
The neighbor's yard sale, etc.
And in a postscript, in another hand,
The death of her dog Hendrix.
She sends by and large the same letter
To eight other people. It is an all-day
Occupation, taken seriously,
Taken to heart.

Une Artiste

She fixed my heart in a collage
And signed me off, *Coeur et courage!*

Red Square

On a mid-winter evening
The brisk changing of the guard,
The long queue at Lenin's tomb,
The glory of St. Basil's,
Now and then a limousine
Speeding into the Kremlin,
Above all, the swirling snow
In the reflection of lights
Like a speckled northern moon,
These images I would send
"With love, and wish you were here."

Arctic Sketchpad

A young fox scampers
At the near wall of a pine wood,
Just full of himself.
A raven comes at dusk to play
Hide and seek.

She rides on runners
Into the sheer, glistening wind.
The dogs are joyful,
The sky blushes above snow fields,
And she laughs.

The mountain appears,
Silver and pink in the dawn.
The tracks of a lynx
Are drawn straight on the blue slope,
A long slant.

The Telling

We will be gone,
But we will have seen
Eternity in the sunrise
And the image of God
In clouds on the mountain.
On the breast of the earth
We will be told of again
In the story of Creation.
In a quiet and seemly way
We will take our places
And be true to the telling.

TG

You brought the essence of a former age
Intact and skillfully upon our stage.
Elizabethans would have honored you
And stirred your passion in their verbal stew.
Then mindful of the present, you brought home
The din of biker bars where vagrants roam,
The blare of bugles in the jazzy night,
Young men dying in the dying light.
And in the workings of your poet's mind,
You struck a balance of delicate kind.
You strove to bring intelligence to bear
Upon inheritance, true, rich, and rare.

The Kiowa No-Face Doll

Kiowa Boarding School, Anadarko

They see how you hold your doll
With love and desperation.
Are they to imagine expression
On the bare, impenetrable mask?
There is nothing to reflect
The face of a child, glad or sad,
Who see upon this sere surface
Anonymity only, a random
Fetish of precise uniformity.
For those who brought you here,
You are the image of your doll.
For those who relegated you
To military sameness, you bear
The visage of a faceless race.

For Bernard Pomerance, in Memory of John Merrick

I am Merrick. Here is my card.
I am with the mutations cross the road.
                    —THE ELEPHANT MAN

In words you have distilled him into pain
Whose every moment, where his head has lain,
Was grave and sinister and full of strain,
A struggle merely to exist in vain.

Summer Song

sweetgrass
a braid burning
     smoke
cupped in the hand
     drawn
to the heart

beyond
summer turns
     simmering
gathering on the curls
of rivers and the lees
     of hummocks

horses
appear on the skyline
there is no prairie sky
     without them
they fasten rain to the earth

autumn stands close by
where the grasses are burned
     at evening
thunder rolls in the gullies
red earth becomes pipestone
     the scent of weather,
like sweetgrass, brings the good of dreams
     and thanksgiving
a summer song

A Sighting

A blue butterfly alighted
On a green leaf beside my hand.
Four times it fluttered away
And returned. That is all.

A Silence Like Frost

A silence like frost hovers here.
I look for the promise of being,
But only the bare presence of death appears.
I think of who I am and do not know.
The God in whom I scarcely believe
Is smug with me, tendering forgiveness,
But as much as I, he is culpable.
Here in these words is no silence broken,
But silence lays a rime upon them,
And, burdened with cold, they die away.

On the wall across from my window
A scarlet leaf spins slowly down,
Touching here and there those that cling
To the dark tangle of their waning life.
It catches the bare edges of light
And rocks into the drift and scatter below.

The Soprano

Untimely was this diva's death.
She found her voice and lost her breath.

Hey

Hey, all you people come together, you hear?
Not for God's sake but for your own.
So you don't all look alike, or dress alike,
Or speak the same language, or have the same religion.

What you do have, all of you, is your human being.
It is the best thing you have or will ever have.
To be human is to be blessed among all creatures,
Free in your spirit and noble in your minds.

Your children come into the world with love,
Love for the plants and animals, for each other.
Do not teach them hatred and violence. Give them
The chance to know and cherish the earth,

The ocean, the dawn, the desert and dusk—
The stories of the world, the mysteries of origin.
Come together and weave the strands of peace
Into an everlasting tapestry of human being.

Bitter Creek Song

Will you go to Bitter Creek tonight?
Will you go to Bitter Creek?
Will you wear the white and yellow dress?
Will your blanket be blue, blue, blue?
There will be dancing by the water.
There will be the courting songs.
Oh, be shy with me tonight, be shy.
But, oh, have eyes for me, for me, for me.
Let your heart whisper to me.
I will breathe the sweetness of your skin.
Will you go to Bitter Creek tonight?
Will you go to Bitter Creek?

An Aspect of Condition

We contemplate the urgency
And engine of our fantasy,

The stars vibrating far and wide,
Abiding on the other side

Of time and distance and remorse.
We would have trade with them of course

And be the ones who dance and play
On silk roads of the Milky Way,

Until we splinter on the bone
And murmur this: we are alone.

Two Figures

These figures moving in my rhyme
Who are they? Death and Death's dog, Time.

Idée Fixe

She harped upon the afterlife
And was therefore a wanting wife.
The here and now were not her wont.
Bemoan her loss; her husband don't.

R.I.P.

He was a sinner and a saint,
And went both ways without restraint.
His mind was said to be chaotic.
Obscure, untidy, and neurotic.

The Mute Intensity of Love

For Barbara

If only I could tell you what you are
And mean to me, I would as well be done
With speech. My urgent words would carry far
Beyond intent and purpose. Only one
Expression would endure therefore, a sigh
And silence all but inarticulate.
The ancient languages of wind comply
With this communion, this profound estate.
For every syllable the heart disdains,
The mute intensity of love remains.

For a Woman Unadorned

It was as if the moon appeared
On a headland of black, bristling trees
Flooding light upon waters below, and
Like the tides beyond, I was summoned
By the gravity of your flesh as it lay,
A fragile suggestion of blood and bone
And all origins of beauty and lust.
You strummed the silver strings of the sea
And made ancient vibrations of music in me.
But, what the hell, you knew that.

The Gardener

The matron of a modern sect,
Here lies a landscape architect.
She bought the farm and now reposes
Among celestial ferns and roses.
God knows a certain air belies her;
Her life was mould and fertilizer.

The Man Who Lost Himself

There was a man who went far away from the town, looking
for salt. On the fourth day of his journey, he suffered great
thirst, and he sat in the shade of a huge rock. In answer to his
prayer, it began to rain. The rain was gentle at first, and the
man's thirst was quenched. But the rain grew hard, and there
was loud thunder and bright lightning. A bolt of lightning
struck the man and wrecked great harm upon him. The man
was blind, and his body was burned and deformed. Somehow
he found his way back home. When the people saw him, they
greeted him with pity and ridicule. He was ashamed of his
blindness and his deformity. In the night he entered into a
holy place and painted stripes on his body and put on a helmet
with horns. The next morning he appeared in the plaza and all
the people were amazed. "Who are you?" they asked. "I am
koshare," he said. "Formerly I was a blind, crippled man. But I
lost myself behind this mask. I am now the being you see
before you, none other. I have brought you salt."

The Artist of Altamira

Another day
The season turned,
The weather burned.
I walked in testaments
Of ancient time.

Another year
The torches blazed,
The bison grazed.
I dwelt in artistry
And paradigm.

Another age,
And darkness rose,
And in repose
My animals remained,
Rude and sublime.

The Modesty of Relics

How just will be my silence when
You look upon my hair and bone,
Reflect upon my grace and then
subvert my meaning to your own.

Of Morning in Spello

In the night I had been dull
and blind, dreaming of nothing.
Now in the brilliant morning
I emerge upon wonder
And see the far cypresses,
the olive groves and onion
fields, the stones of Umbria.
I am myself an essence,
a green splinter of the sun.
I shall eat a bursting fig.
I shall pass a dead man's door.
I shall be glad to inhabit
the thin invisible air,
the bright prism of summer.

Prayer to the Mind

O mind, good mind, O blessed mind,
Succeed the body, be so kind.

The Bone Striker*

My footprints are those of a beast,
The bear, the buffalo, the wolf.
My voice is that of the whirlwind,
The gathering of a prairie storm.
My song is that of a warrior,
The song of the Bone Striker.

I carry the ball of bone.
I stand my ground and strike,
I stand my ground and strike.
I stand my ground,
I stand my ground.

I boast,
I boast in the presence of my enemy.
I boast in the presence of death.
Face me, for I am the Bone Striker.
Face me.
Face me.

* The Bone Strikers were the members of an early military society in the Kiowa tribe. Each man carried a large bone, which he used as a club. The Bone Strikers banded together in battle and stood their ground to the death.

The Wheel

Where wind sifts glitter from the drifts,
And deer regard you without fear
And stand like the stumps about them,
Motionless, tawny with a late gleaming
Of the November sun, cross into wilderness.
And recall imperfectly your severance
From this far, forgotten world,
And contemplate the riddle of your return.

Then enter upon the wheel
With bare recognition and acute respect,
The mere acceptance of the unintelligible.
Forsake the cellular memory of hopelessness.
Move among the spokes and cairns.
Then take your heart away, keeping
The beats of a Creation song, a paean
To the alien, savage swell.

Eclipse

Novosibirsk, 2008

From Mongolia the Ob,
Flowing north to the Arctic,
Slants into the white city
Bearing a traffic I know—
Asian merchants, seal hunters,
Old people of the taiga.
Lord, let us see what is there.

Now summer on the bright beach;
The sky is clear. Everyone
Is high on expectation.
And then the quiet havoc;
The edge of the moon intrudes
Upon an old deity,
Lord, let us see what is there.

And dark streams writhe on the sand.
Primal light itself recedes,
And fear in the ancient guise
Of darkness enters the caves
Of the brain. A ring of fire
Describes a perfect black disc.
Lord, let us see what is there.

The great river roils slowly
In the gleam of dawn or dusk.
For a time, time holds no sway.
Shadows take hold of the light
And pass. The afternoon,
Barely diminished, goes on.
Lord, let us see what is there.

Sobre Mesa

Did you chip the calf, Alfredo?
Sí, I chipped the calf, Jose.
Did you ride with your knees, Alfredo?
With my knees and heart, Jose.
Did your horse sling his head, Alfredo?
Sí, his head was slung low, Jose.
Did he see into the calf's eyes, Alfredo?
Sí, he saw into the eyes, Jose.
What did he see there, Alfredo?
Nada. There was nothing to see, Jose.
You have a fine cutting horse, Alfredo.
Sí, mine is a fine cutting horse, Jose.
Por favor, have one more, Alfredo.
Sí, gracias, Jose, one more for the ride.

Vision Quest

Four days I lived on tea and sage
And dreamed in symbols of an age,
A beast incising on the tree:
I am the bear Tsoai-talee.

The Scraps of Praise

Do not believe them. They are lies.
They are the critic's enterprise.

But if you must, take each scrap in,
Imagining what might have been.

And if you listen to yourself,
All lies grow dusty on the shelf.

Write little and write well, I say,
And be the bard for whom you pray.

Song of the Conqueror

Rejoice in the illusive spoils of peace,
And grant to greed the order of surcease;
Revel in want, and may your tribe decrease.

Elemental Speech

Lover, be my mime,
And let your fingertips touch
What they will of me.
I am at your disposal.

Are you trembling?
Do I feel you tense your toes?
Will you wind your hair
Around me like vagrant smoke?

Do you taste of salt,
Like herring eggs on seaweed
And the damp of you
At the creases of your limbs?

So you invent speech.
Your guttural responses
Are an intercourse
Now and then. I take your meaning.

A West Side Drinking Song

I speak of your dementia
And hear in it my own.
And, old friend, in absentia,
We trace the whole unknown.

Old friend, sobriety
Would surely drive us sane.
Be done with sanity.
It is a dreadful bane.

Old friend, let us restore
Compassion to the mind.
One for the road, and for
Such wit as we can find.

First Voyage

Again the far morning; we come to this,
The edge of earth, beyond which nothing is.
Between worlds, in the close of stagnant time,
The air is warm, sea-scented, and benign.

Tonight we shall be dead in the water,
And dead the reckoning from this quarter,
A doubtful flickering of inland light—
A buoyant star, bobbing, remote and bright.

I Canot Wrt

I canot wrt the sog I wsh t sin,

Fr al t t in Chn

My lve i detles, n my hrt i pur

N Cotn Ee Jo he tke t cur

Whoa

The Mortal Memory

You died in the lunar eclipse.
I think you might have been at peace;
I could not read you in your sleep

At such times mere intention slips
Beyond intention's grasp. Hours cease,
And only love is in our keep.

I love you though you are not here,
A love inconstant, faint, and sere.

To Tell You of My Love*

Eh neh neh neh,
Oh, my beloved:

I tell you of my love,
You listen, you listen.
I whisper you my love,
You listen, you listen.

Now hear my words falling like snow
Upon your hair. Beloved, know
My song returns your deepest dream,
My breath the lucent soul you seem.

Eh neh neh neh,
Oh, my beloved.

My words run as rainwater runs
Upon your skin. Like winter suns
The stars touch wonder to your face,
I pray the blessing of your grace.

Eh neh neh neh,
Oh, my beloved.

* The exclamation, "Eh neh neh neh," is a Kiowa formula, used most often by
Kiowa women. It registers conviction or acknowledgment of that which is
wondrous.

About Me Like a Robe*

For that man sees that I am beautiful;
I will dust my skin with pollen and sage.

For that man sings to me in lonesome strains;
I will pretend to hear the river roll.

For that man lingers late about my camp;
I will look beyond him, as if dreaming.

For he brings my mother glittering beads;
I will count them, reckoning his intent.

For he boasts to my father of his deeds;
I will laugh and make faces behind him.

For he gives strawberries to my sister;
I will chide him for being lost in love.

For that man tells me stories from his heart;
I will wear them about me like a robe.

* This is a courting song, sung by the woman courted. She chides her suitor
with delicious irony.

Little Newborn, Sleep*

Little newborn, the blackbirds are calling;
How they call upon your sleep.

Little newborn, the river is rolling;
How it runs upon your sleep.

Little newborn, the long winds are turning;
How they wheel upon your sleep.

Little newborn, the old bear is creeping;
How he bends upon your sleep.

On the purple mountain we are dancing,
Among the living trees we are dancing.

We dance in your dreams, we play in your dreams.
We dance and play in the field of your dreams.

Sleep, little newborn, you are welcome here.
Sleep, little newborn, sleep peacefully here.

* Lullabys are sung to soothe babies and young children. They are the singing of the earth and its creatures. They instill calm and serenity in the child. They express the innocence of the child and nurture the child's spirit. They welcome the child into the world.

A Cradle for This Child*

This child who draws so near,
Who has no name, who cannot see,
Who waits in darkness to be born
Into an empty world,
I make a cradle for this child.

This child whose trust we keep,
Who knows of nothing but our love,
Whose hands will guide our destiny
Into an empty world,
I make a cradle for this child.

This child who blesses us,
Whose words will heal and carry on
Beyond the silence of our sorrow,
Beyond an empty world,
I make a cradle for this child.

This child who will enter
Among us in our empty world
And stand before us in our need
And promise us the dawn,
I make a cradle for this child.

* In the middle of the nineteenth century, when the Plains Indians had nearly
lost all hope, the women began to make cradle boards—beautiful beaded works
of art—for the unborn children. It was their way of vesting one last hope for a
future, for survival itself.

The Middle Distance

Imagine the space between here and there.
Vision holds upon an aura of the earth,
And on that nebulous band a bird appears.

It takes shape in the vagaries of light,
Becoming wholly its own definition.
It hangs inherently there, opposite the air.

Less the image, more the beholding it, is true,
A perception of the wild that is wild itself.

This is an isolation that confirms the alien eye,
The bird, alone, appearing on the transparent field,
The middle distance.

Woman in the Plain: A Portrait

Behold her in the foreground. She takes shape
In the long light, imaging the unknown.
She moves in weavings of the prairie grass,
Her motion slow and undulant, almost

A dance, indeed almost a ritual.
Among broken stoneworks, against the sky,
She seems always to be, embodied here
In this bright field, in possibility.

Momently concentrated, she is borne
On the echoes of the wind, in the mind
Of soil and summer. Behold what she is,
And, veiled in art, what she appears to be.

A Woman Beyond Words

You had become your metaphor, yourself
Read in my play of words and passages.
I defined you; you were the utterance
I made when first I set my mind on forms
Traditional and modern, on language
For its own sake.
                          Now you exceed my reach.
You will not be contained in my best lines.
Good riddance. Go your way ineffably.

Winter Arcs

A poet stands
among smoking stones
and cold waterfalls.
He thinks of nothing,
and yet the faint impulse
to tell of Creation
comes upon him.
The story is too large
for a couplet
or even a quatrain.
Dumb with wonder,
he beholds rainbows
and the random fishes
that rise and freeze,
iridescent on the air.

A Parable of Snails

They inch so lightly on the walk.
Their trails glisten in the moonlight.
They contemplate each blade and stalk
And pray the mysteries of night.

They listen in their house of leaves
And hear the voices of the dead.
Their congress is a loom that weaves
The tapestries of holy dread.

What do they know of time and change?
What drives their will to come and go
Along a wild and ancient range
Of being that we cannot know?

Beyond their knowing is the loss
Of boundaries they cannot cross.

The Trace

Behold the pale streak of stars
Above the black line of land
Where evening edges the night.
Is it the path of the dead
Who danced with us in summer
And did not speak of roaming?
Neither do we speak of it,
But we scan the gleaming trace.

Crazy Dog Song

Over me the sun
Under me the earth
My life is good
It ought not to be better
That I should stand fast

A Farther Home

An old, deranged woman in a chair:
You think that she has never been composed,
That as a child she embodied age and wrath.
She emits a scream inside herself.
It is a visible scream, inaudible and terrible.
It is mute, merely motion in the wind
Of a farther place, the homeland of her heart.

We Have Seen the Animals

Lascaux

For we have seen the animals
That linger in primordial dark,
Parade in step and intervals
That mark millennia, an arc

Of time beyond the reckoning.
Whose hand has traced these living lines?
Whose mind has ventured past the thing
That mere mortality confines?

Horse, bison, auroch, bear, and deer,
Convene forever in the night,
Their ghosts, in old communion here,
Emerge in stark, forgotten light.

Or has their spirit thrived unseen,
Bled into earth and rock?—
In attitudes austere, serene,
Evincing myth, story, epoch.

Sternenwandler

After a painting by Emil Nolde

Time is static on the void, and see,
A man wanders among the stars.

He does not transcend the picture plane,
But hovers in a greatcoat, in oblivion,

In the astral, pulsing sea, in silence,
Imperturbable and indifferent.

Time is static on the void, illumined.
The man stands beyond and ever there.

Before and farther than the reach implies,
I bear his ghost; I am his compromise.

The Death of a Ceramicist

Here lies the potter Tim O'Dea,
Who has himself become his clay,
And lest his mem'ry be forgot,
Recycle him into a pot.

Visitors

They came
Not to see us
But to see themselves in our eyes
And our demise
And in the blood on their hands

Now we think it was
They saw into a twisting wind
And were blinded

We dance and the earth quakes
We dance and the earth quakes

The grasses lie low
And the earth quakes

Esquire

Beneath this stone a lawyer lies.
And lying led to his demise.
He labored in precincts judicial.
And strove to make his lies official.
"Justice is my life," he said,
But nonetheless the man is dead.

Of the Ghost Dance

I circle above
The burial grounds of the earth
I lay my feathers on the wind
And fly

Consolation in Fives and Sevens

In the time of strife,
a dream of order begins.
At first there is light,
and objects break from the field.
Then color and shape;
a wedge of migrating birds
finds old alignments
of motion and grace. Thickets
emerge in vapor
by rivers that curl to seas,
crazing distances.
The music of morning wind
on the plaited grass
touches the ear with whispers
of the earth turning,
and the whole is as it is,
imperturbable.

The Bearers

They come not often now, the ones who bear
The emblems of old enmities and strife.
Now that I am at ease with age, I see,
As in a glass upon a photograph,
Their sad mimicry and reflecting gaze,
Their vague and seldom forms dismembering.
How they strive to assemble, to take shape!
They blur in being, drift in vortices
Of time, and mouth the silence of their names.

19 rue de Lille

Across the courtyard light ascends
And will ascend to night. Below
Are windows flickering. Time bends
Beyond the solar afterglow.

I hunt the moon, imagine seas
That reach to dawns appearing. Here,
In this dark street, and as I please,
I quest upon the astral sphere.

To Tangle

I would propose,
Puppy Eyes,
That we tangle tonight.
The moon is right
And the air is scented with sweetgrass.
Listen. Do you hear
How my words are tangled
In the notes of my flute?
And I am mute,
And your hair is scented with clover.
I will enfold you
In a robe of sunrise colors,
And we will tangle smoke
In the stars.

A Song of Thanksgiving

Your name is spoken in the camps
We make a song for you
  In our song there is honor
  In our song there is respect
  In our song there is affection
  In our song there is thanksgiving
Our words are borne northward
Our words bear you on your quest

Your name is spoken in the camps
We make a dance for you
  In our dance there is gladness
  In our dance there is laughter
  In our dance there is communion
  In our dance there is fulfillment
Our words are borne westward
Our words bear you on your quest

Your name is spoken in the camps
We make a prayer for you
  In our prayer there is power
  In our prayer there is well-being
  In our prayer there is humility
  In our prayer there is transcendence
Our words are borne southward
Our words bear you on your quest

Your name is spoken in the camps
We make a vision for you
  In our vision there is wonder
  In our vision there is beauty
  In our vision there is peace
  In our vision there is sunrise
Our words are borne eastward
Our words bear you on your quest

An Honor Song in the Old Style

For Vine Deloria, Jr.

Where words were first shaped
Into sacred bundles and placed
On altars of earth and stone
We made prayers of thanksgiving
      glad to have been summoned
      glad to have been given names
      glad to have been touched by the sun
      glad to have heard the silence

Where visions were first borne
upon sacred winds and glittered
on the darkness of our camps
we sang of our well-being
      proud to have been summoned
      proud to have named our destiny
      proud to have spoken the sunrise
      proud to have broken the silence

Where thunder rolled across the world
and rain rattled on the ancient trails
and on the shadows of origin
we danced the days of our dreaming
      whole in the summons of life
      whole in the names of our deities
      whole in the radiance of the sun
      whole in the silence of the stars

Aho

The Herd

Theirs is the shape of shade, grass braids
burned, black bleedings of the earth,
the crust of the Malpais.
They shimmer beyond relief;
they move and seem not to move,
inexorable as birth,
irresistible as death.

Theirs is the sound of thunder,
of rain dancing to the dawn,
of the song of origin
and the round running of winds.
Their passing is an omen
always beyond mere meaning,
always ominous and there.

Animal shield of the sun,
they bear darkness on the plain,
an endless curve of seasons
in which they persist. They stay,
seemingly available
to the mind's eye, seemingly
present in the vision's range.

When at last they graze away,
only the faint impression
of their having been remains—
some estimate of loss, some
sorrow of the soil. The ghost
of their image is therefore
made whole and original.

The Dead of Winter

I.

I know the winter. Cold and dark decree
The round of seasons. Solstices imply
The other side of mute eternity:
To bear, to burn, to wither, and to die.

2.

These silent winter days derange the fields,
And ravens call upon the placid sky.
Night rises with the cold, and order yields.
Stars tremble overhead, arc, flare, and die.

3.

Again the deep evening, another time.
Old voices come to me across the way.
Muffled in snow, they seem almost to mime
My wonder, but I know not what they say.

There is no solace in them, but they drift
Among the branches and the vines. They sigh
And wane into these whispers that I sift
Into sleep. There they rattle and they die.

Notebook

As a child I remarked the world in scrawls of wonder. And so do I now in the envy of age.

I dare to write of myself. I am my good subject. Besides, imaginings, not facts, are at issue. Imagination is the soul of the self.

To be or not to be besotted with words. There is the rub; but for the poet there is no question; there is only passion and mandate.

I have discovered that among the best of all healings is deep, dreamless sleep, to be still and mindless in the suspension of time.

And time is an illusion. We move through a dimension we call time, but we cannot believe in it.

Beyond every tree on the plain is a clear dawn and eternity.

In my best memory there are geese in the sky and horses beyond the river. It is winter, and snow is falling. I am becoming alive to the world. I have no words for this awakening, only a quiet beyond language.

Do I deserve the insights that come to me in the night and day? Perhaps, for they are the stepping stones that lead to wisdom, the divine confusion we call reality.

I have lived a longer time than most people on the earth. Am I therefore wise? Yes, I must believe so, for I have read the sacred signs, and they indicate that I have lived a longer time than have most people on the earth.

I have seen three things that I do not expect to see again: a double rainbow of extraordinary brilliance above the *Malpais*; a night sky at Lukachukai bearing countless stars so close to earth as to stun the senses; and a sunset at Chinle, in which literally half the dome of the sky was a conflagration beyond imagining. It strikes me now that these things were ephemeral and beyond my comprehension. That is appropriate, I think. Such things should not remain to be known too well, and they should occur in the realm of infinity.

What is it that demands sorrow and gladness of us? The balance of being, perhaps, on the scales of God.

Be still. What is the good of clocking eternity?

Indifferent and overwhelming is the sea. It is a plane for fools and heroes and lovers of the unknown.

Yes, I was that very boy who dreamed of animals and birds, and of the magic of the word, the majesty of the poem, the solace of the song.

I drove along the edge of a caldera, and a red-tail hawk appeared suddenly and sailed beside me, its feathers rippling and iridescent, in close formation. It was as if we had the same appointment with the setting sun.

For some years now I have lived with a mystery: who is the man known as Cotton-eye Joe? Where does he come from, and where does he go?

Rain at Altamira, and a winding walk to the green door in the hillside. On this side time, on the other side, timelessness. When we emerged we could not speak, so hard was the hold of eternity.

You stepped out of the abandoned Hogan, beheld the towering butte, and said, "So, you are still there."

The verb *to be* and the *zero*, the concepts of existence and nothingness. Are these not the bookends of everything?

On the Moscow Metro we caught sight of each other, and in the long rattle of transport our eyes met and glanced away several times. It was an unworthy propriety. You were a beautiful woman, I a reader of signs. You gave me one last glance as you stepped out at Krasnopresnenskaya. It was surely an invitation. Why on earth did I not accept, then and there? What direction might my life have taken? When I excluded you I was excluded.

I was playing the part of a bear. You were fascinated. We became lovers. It is a whole story.

Beneath my window are children waiting for the school bus in the northern dark. When they are gone the light of day appears by degrees. A raven plays with a young red fox on the near edge of the wood. The raven has by far the advantage, but the fox has more fun.

You emitted a laugh that carried to the farthest room, the very one in which *War and Peace* was written. Yet it was nearly modest and discreet. Everyone fell silent. When we went, in a horse-drawn wagon, to Tolstoy's grave, we knew that we had come to a milestone in the history of Russia and of literature. Somewhere in the grass, or under a century of dead leaves, lies the green stick that, as a child, Leo Nikolaevich thought would bring peace to the world.

For almost three quarters of a century, every morning a new world.

On a portal of the Gur Emir in Arabic: "He who has seen Tamerlane's tomb has seen the world." I confirm that this is true.

"Write little and write well," he said.

I have taken a thousand photographs, more, but one I took in Moscow thirty years ago—a woman at a window—is worth all the others to me. Perhaps the capture of such moments is the signature of the soul.

On the Ob at dusk we landed on a small island where some men were cooking fish for our dinner. The sky was streaked with soft colors. It was almost cold, and the fire was delicious. I was composing a poem in my mind.

One night in Andalucía, we had the Alhambra to ourselves. We wandered through the exquisite gardens, the more than elaborate architecture, and we stood on the massive walls, looking down at the glittering lights of Granada below. And didn't we see firelight flickering in the caves and hear the gypsies singing?

The village. The smell of piñon and juniper smoke. A black storm descending into the canyon. Posole simmering. All is well.

Near Minto, on the way to Susan's dog camp, a lynx moving diagonally across the field of snow.

In Saucelito. In a restaurant overlooking the Bay, a woman in a wide-brimmed yellow hat, wearing long yellow gloves. I knew her taste. Wine and chicken livers with eggs. Something of French Impressionism, surely.

"I tried," I said. "The angels can't do more," the nun said. But in my heart I knew the angels could do more.

From my window in the Marina I can see the great divide at the foot of Fillmore Street and the great ships passing by. And in the night, rain making beautiful, distorted reflections of the lights in Cow Hollow. Fog horns.

Wet grasses about his feet, and the sun's rays streaking down. Above Rainy Mountain a cloud like smoke, and below a camp. Tepees tall and white, like great migrating birds. That is what *Tso-odle* saw as a boy. *Ah-keah-de*, they were camping.

My walking stick is made of hickory and has a fine crook to it. There is a small knot inside the crook, a kind of kernel that fits the hand nicely to the heft and balance. It would benefit a blind man, taking hold of it before going out of doors. The stick is old and substantial. A genuine antique, telling of another age and style. The shaft is not round but octagonal, fashioned with considerable care and patience. Along one of the eight surfaces there are numerous, miniscule markers, signifying a count, perhaps. One might think of Sitting Bull, counting the hundred strips of flesh that he cut from his arm before the Battle of the Little Bighorn. The stick was once painted red. You can see the pigment, like old berry stains, here and there. The man who gave it to me said that he had got it from an old people's home at Pine Ridge. I feel that I know the man to whom it once belonged. I have felt the grip of his hand in my own.

The white blossoms of pear trees and the slashes of red earth in the grasses, the brown rivers high and roiling. The sky is the very blue of serenity, and the horizons are so far away as to exceed the reach of vision. But here, just here, is a small bird hopping.

The Rolling

Where, beyond the mind's reach, words rained down on the long beach and the waves, each one an element of thunder, we made love and could not speak. Words were not yet in our keeping; they were emerging, just, from a place of origin. It seemed that the love we made was older then the words. But the words, like thunder, rolled and were innumerable with the turning and returning waves.

CPSIA information can be obtained
at www.ICGtesting.com
Printed in the USA
LVHW05s0733110918
589697LV00001B/16/P